Business as Usual Or is it?

Thoughts on being successful in business.

Advice is seldom welcome;
and those who want it the most
always like it the least.

Philip Dormer Stanhope

Compiled by Melba T. Sparrow

Published by Melba T. Sparrow in association with
Marblehead Publishing, Raleigh, North Carolina

For additional copies of this book contact:
    Melba T. Sparrow
    Sparrow Construction Co., Inc.
    P. O. Box 33609
    Raleigh, NC 27636
    (919) 833-7342

Printed in the United States of America

Library of Congress Catalog Card Number:
99-60833

ISBN: 0-943335-13-2

I dedicate this book to my husband, J. Ray Sparrow, who has managed his business with integrity and has set high standards and a fine example for those who wish to enter the business world.

Table of Contents

Foreword

Why Assemble Wise Sayings to Produce a Book?

As an executive of the Sparrow Construction Co., Inc. in Raleigh, NC, Melba Sparrow soon learned that being a problem solver for employees required her to be authentic, self-motivated and responsive to the needs of others.

To help others, Melba knew that acceptance of change is one of life's constants. Collecting adages, aphorisms, and quotations from literature as well as words of wisdom from successful business men and women gave her a broader outlook on the situations that executives, managers and workers face.

Melba has succeeded in finding a balance in her business and personal life. She has been inspired by the words of leaders in the fields of business, philosophy and government.

Reading the thoughts expressed in these pages also can stimulate your thinking and that of your employees. All of you may find answers to some of the challenges facing you in your business.

Helen Haft Goldstein

Preface

"The ideas I stand for are not mine. I borrowed them
from Socrates. I swiped them from Chesterfield. I stole
them from Jesus. And I put them in a book. If you don't
like their rules, whose would you use?"

> Dale Carnegie, on his book,
> *How to Win Friends and
> Influence People,* quoted in
> *Newsweek,* August 8, 1955

Acknowledgments

A special thank you to Helen Haft Goldstein who guided me and shared her self, her time and experience with me. She encouraged me to proceed and make the time to follow my dream.

Rules for Good Business

1. Customers are the lifeblood of any business.
2. Business is dependent on customers and their goodwill.
3. Every person is a potential customer.
4. Customers are people who expect advice, help and attention.
5. Do not ignore customers; be attentive.
6. Never argue with a customer; just listen to what he or she has to say.
7. Be courteous at all times, even if the customer seems to be rude.
8. Remember that the most important person in any business is the customer.

Source Unknown

A little bit of *quality* will always make them smile;
A little bit of *courtesy* will bring them in a mile;
A little bit of *friendliness* will tickle them 'tis plain—
And a little bit of *service* will bring them back again.

Anonymous

To carry on a successful business, a man must have imagination. He must see things as in a vision, a dream of the whole thing.

Charles Schwab

The successful business man sometimes makes his money by ability and experience; but he generally makes it by mistake.

Gilbert K. Chesterton

It is not the crook in modern business that we fear but the honest man who does not know what he is doing.

Owen D. Young

We demand that big business give the people a square deal; in return we must insist that when anyone engaged in big business honestly endeavors to do right, he shall himself be given a square deal.

Theodore Roosevelt Autobiography, 1913

In business, the earning of profit is something more than an incident of success. It is an essential condition of success. It is an essential condition of success because the continued absence of profit itself spells failure.

Supreme Court Justice Louis D. Brandeis

Every great man of business has got somewhere a touch of the idealist in him.

Woodrow Wilson

Managing Your Business by Delegating

1. **Keep an assignment log**
   When you delegate a task, write it down. Then you can check employees' progress periodically and take action, if necessary.

2. **Develop a workable reporting system with deadlines**
   This could be weekly meetings with employees, or monthly reports. Employees will feel accountable for the completion of their tasks.

3. **Establish concrete objectives that can be measured**
   Be specific, so employees will feel confident in making decisions on their own.

4. **Stress the results of the assigned task, not details**
   Tell your employees that it is the final outcome of the assignment that concerns you, not the day-to-day progress that is being made.

5. **Don't give solutions to problems; foster questions**
   Don't solve employees' problems for them; teach
   them how to find possible answers for themselves.

6. **Take the abilities of employees into account**
   Assign jobs which a person can handle well. His
   talents and personality should be equal to the task.

Source Unknown

**Executive: an individual who directs or controls an
organization; one who holds a position of
administrative responsibility.**

The business executive is by profession a decision
maker. Uncertainty is his opponent. Overcoming it is
his mission. Whether the outcome is a consequence of
luck or of wisdom, the moment of decision is without
doubt the most creative and critical event in the life of
the executive.

J. McDonald, "Businessmen Make Decisions,"
Fortune, *August 1955*

A successful executive in business is the one who can delegate all the responsibility, shift all the blame, and appropriate all the credit.

A business genius is a man who knows the difference between being let in on a deal and taken in on one.

A good business manager hires optimists as salesmen and pessimists to run the credit department.

Executive ability is a talent for deciding something quickly and getting someone else to do it.

A good executive is judged by the company he keeps— solvent.

Sources Unknown

Manager: One who has executive skills and supervises something, such as a business; a person whose work or profession is management

Every supervisor has his own domain in which he is manager, leader, negotiator, mentor, counselor, judge, coach, team player, therapist and cheerleader. He wears many hats, and in addition, his job requires that he manage projects, decide on priorities, and interact with employees and other people.

Goals which managers share with executives:
1. Attract more customers
2. Make a better product
3. Render better service
4. Improve working relationships

How to achieve these goals
1. Believe in what you are doing
2. Be enthusiastic—it's contagious
3. Be friendly and smile often
4. Let everyone know that you are enjoying yourself at work

Source Unknown

Civilization and profits go hand in hand.

Calvin Coolidge, 1920

Have confidence that if you have done a little thing well, you can do a bigger thing well too.

Storey

If once you forfeit the confidence of your fellow citizens, you can never regain their respect and esteem.

Abraham Lincoln

The best soldier does not attack. The superior fighter succeeds without violence. The greatest conqueror wins without a struggle. The most successful manager leads without dictating. This is called intelligent nonaggressiveness. This is called mastery of men.

Lao-Tsu, Toa Teh King

The best way for any business to keep on the upgrade is to stay on the level.

Business is made good by yearning, learning and earning.

The best way to go into business is with high hopes and low overhead.

Business is a lot like tennis—those who don't serve well wind up losing.

Honesty is one business policy that will never have to be changed to keep up with the times.

If you want to go far in business, you'll have to stay close to it.

Business know-how is when a fellow knows his business and what's none of his business.

It isn't the number of people employed in a business that makes it successful, it's the number working.

Sources Unknown

If A equals success, then the formula is A equals X plus Y and Z, with X being work, Y play, and Z keeping your mouth shut.

Albert Einstein

We work not only to produce but to give value to time. Where one's work is concerned, one should be an epicure.

Delacroix

We succeed in enterprises which demand the positive qualities we possess, but we excel in those which can also make use of our defects.

Toqueville

Money-getters are the benefactors of our race. To them we are indebted for our institutions of learning, and of art, our academies, colleges and churches.

P.T. Barnum

If a man has good corn, or wood, or boards, or pigs to sell or can make better chairs or knives, crucibles, or church organs better than anybody else, you will find a broad hard-beaten road to his house, even though it be in the woods.

Ralph Waldo Emerson

Business without profit is not business any more than a pickle is a candy.

Charles F. Abbott

Business has only two basic functions—marketing and innovation.

Peter Drucker

Business more than any other occupation is a continual dealing with the future; it is a continual calculation, an instinctive exercise in foresight.

Anonymous

There are two times in a man's life when he should not speculate: when he can't afford it and when he can.

Mark Twain

Wisdom from the Past

My stronger guilt defeats my strong intent; And, like a man to double business bound, I stand in pause where I shall first begin, And both neglect.

Shakespeare's Hamlet

My rule always was to do business of the day in the day.

Duke of Wellington, 1835

Men in great places are thrice servants: servants of the state, servants of fame, and servants of business.

Francis Bacon, 17th century

To business that we love we rise betime, And go to with delight.

Shakespeare

Cecil's despatch of business was extraordinary, his maxim being: "The shortest way to do many things is to do only one thing at once."

Samuel Smiles

I must create a system, or be enslaved by another man's; I will not reason and compare; my business is to Create.

William Blake

In civil business: what first, boldness?; what second and third? boldness; and yet boldness is a child of ignorance and baseness. Boldness is an ill keeper of promise.

Francis Bacon

There is nothing more requisite in business than dispatch.

Joseph Addison

Who first invented Work—and tied the free
And holy-day rejoicing spirit down
To the ever-haunting importunity
Of Business, in the green fields, and the town—
To plough, loom, anvil, spade, and, oh, most sad,
To this dry drudgery of the desk's dead wood?

Charles Lamb

O! that a man might know
The end of this day's Business, ere it come;
But it sufficeth that the day will end;
And then the end is known.

Shakespeare's Julius Caesar

"No Business before breakfast, Glum!" says the King,
"Breakfast first, Business next."

William Makepeace Thackeray

Description of Successful People
(courtesy of H. K. Dugdale and Trico Drywall)

1. They have plenty of drive
People who go places in their work usually have almost tireless energy—or drive. They work persistently toward their objective.

2. They accept responsibility cheerfully
Responsibility is a challenge to our ability and to our attitude toward our work. Smart people not only welcome it but seek it as the best way to prove their value.

3. They know that success is never an accident
It is not a matter of "luck"—but of doing those things which experience teaches are most likely to lead to success. A successful person is one who makes it a habit to do the things which failures habitually try to avoid doing.

4. They know that the customer is their real "boss"

Customers are the life blood of a business—its most valuable asset. Without them there would be no business, no jobs. Your company is judged by the quality and value of everything it does. See that you do your best to uphold its standards and help to hold its customers.

5. They Look-Listen-and Learn

To understand what goes on around us we must keep our eyes, ears, and minds open. There is a difference between seeing and observing—hearing and under- standing. Our eyes and ears are supply routes to the brain—but if our minds are closed to new ideas, nothing gets through. Keep on the alert.

6. They find out—if they're not sure

It is always better to make sure than to make a mistake. No one will excuse that lamest of all alibis, "I didn't know." If you don't know, find out.

7. They set an example to others

In striving to do a better job yourself—see that you inspire and encourage those around you to follow your example. You are all members of the same team.

8. They know that the next field only looks greener

The place to succeed is where you are—not in some other job or company. The man who thinks he can't succeed in his present job has simply failed to look for and discover the many opportunities for becoming more valuable where he is. His job can become a gold mine if he just digs beneath the surface.

9. They welcome new ideas

New ideas are the seeds of progress—and change accepted order today. When we refuse to accept ideas, we cease to grow. Welcome them, give them consideration. Never be afraid to change.

10. They profit by their mistakes

No one ever mastered any undertaking without making mistakes along the way. It is as important to know what not to do as what to do. Our mistakes help us and enable us to help others avoid them.

11. They speak clearly and convincingly

In business we must be able to get our ideas across and make our instructions understood in order to avoid misunderstandings, delays and errors. Be brief—be definite—say exactly what you mean.

12. They don't expect all the credit

Haven't you noticed that people who do things that count, never stop to count them? Instead of expecting a lot of credit and applause, they keep trying to make what they do tomorrow count even more. No good work goes unnoticed.

13. They cooperate

Instead of playing it alone—they pitch in and cooperate, realizing that which is best for the team, is best for the company—and for them. There is no room in business for "lone wolves" and "prima donnas."

14. They take responsibility for their own future

The company you work for is not responsible for your future progress, nor is the job you hold in the company. You and you alone determine how far up the success ladder you will climb.

15. They think things through—FIRST

No man was ever fired for saying, "I'll think it over." It is always better to be right than sorry. Take time to think things through—the more important the decision, the less need for hurry.

16. They believe that good manners are good business

"Manners mark the man" and "We cannot always oblige, but we can always speak obligingly." Courtesy, consideration and tact add up to good manners and they not only help us, but they stimulate and encourage those around us.

17. They know the world does not owe them a living

Instead, they feel that they owe "the world" the very best of which they are capable—and that "the world" will reward them accordingly.

18. They are willing to go that "extra mile"

The people most likely to succeed are not the chronic clock watchers—but that more exclusive group—the "extra milers,"—the men and women who gladly do whatever is necessary to be of value. Did you ever notice how many executives take briefcases home with them?

19. They are careful about their finances

A man who spends beyond his means seldom is a good employee and usually blames his employer for his money troubles. Too much debt—over extravagance—no constructive savings plan all lead to trouble, worry and lack of efficiency on the job. Don't try to keep up with the Joneses—and do save regularly, if only a little.

20. They set a goal for themselves

Such people have an objective, a sense of direction. They know where they want to go and are willing to study, work and save in order to get there, stead of trusting to luck. They know that no one can go higher than he thinks he can.

21. They know that anything worth having has a price tag

There is a price tag on success. Like everything of value, it has to be paid for in personal effort. Nothing is free—not even failure—for the price of failure is success itself.

22. They keep physically and mentally fit

They realize that a high level of physical and mental energy is essential, if one is to maintain the tempo of modern business.

23. They earnestly want to succeed

Most people are half-hearted about it. It is said that only about 10% of working people really want to succeed, and have done something about it. An attitude of indifference produces an indifferent result. When we finally realize that the company's success is reflected in our own success, we put our best into everything we do.

24. They know the value of enthusiasm

Haven't you noticed that enthusiasm is a magic spark that inspired an entire department, company, or community? It breeds confidence and courage in everyone within its radius. Be enthusiastic about your job and your organization, and everything it stands for.

25. They make others feel important

Every job in your company is important and it follows that every worker is important too. Never belittle a fellow worker, or his job. Avoid criticism—especially before others. Make a person feel important and you will win a loyal friend.

26. They try to help the boss

He is an important person, or he wouldn't be the boss. He has his problems too—many more than those under his supervision. By doing your own job better, you help him to do a better job, and that helps the company.

27. They never "Pass the Buck"

If they make a mistake—forget instructions—are late for work or an appointment, they admit it and take full blame instead of trying to blame someone else.

28. They control their temper

A quick temper or sarcastic tongue has closed the door to success for many an otherwise able man. Be tactful, slow to anger, and don't condemn another behind his back.

29. They never forget...

that good enough is not good enough today and that only your best will pass the test.

30. They consider work a privilege, not a chore

Many people complain when they are unemployed, but many complain at having to work at all and consider working a burden. Work is a privilege—an opportunity to be of service and thus justify one's right to exist. The more mature the man, the more grateful he is for work.

31. They are their own critic

Always check your own work carefully, before passing it on. Be sure that everything you do measures up to your own standard and the company's standards.

32. They've learned that "easy does it"

You'll live longer, enjoy your work more, and do vastly better work if you work calmly and steadily. "Take it easy" does not mean "loaf on the job," but "take time to do it right."

33. They try to cut expenses

Every step in the operation of a business costs money. By eliminating unnecessary steps we save time and money and thus become more valuable to the company. Keep your eyes open for ways to cut expenses without sacrificing quality.

Opportunities are usually disguised by hard work, so most people don't recognize them.

Ann Landers

Business is a combination of war and sport.

Andre Maurols

Every young man would do well to remember that all successful business stands on the foundation of morality.

Henry Ward Beecher

If we devote our time disparaging the products of our business rivals, we hurt business generally, reduce confidence, and increase discontent.

Edward N. Hurley

Many persons have an idea that one cannot be in business and lead an upright life, whereas the truth is that no one succeeds in business to any great extent, who misleads or misrepresents.

John Wanamaker

Anybody can cut prices, but it takes brains to make a better article.

Philip D. Armour

All business proceeds on beliefs, or judgment of probabilities, and not on certainties.

Charles Eliot

The world is filled with willing people; some willing to work, the rest willing to let them.

Robert Frost

Patience is a most necessary quality for business. Many a man would rather you heard his story than grant his request.

Chesterfield

Men of business must not break their word twice.

Thomas Fuller

There are an enormous number of managers who have retired on the job.

Anonymous

Management by objectives works if you know the objectives. Ninety percent of the time you don't.

Peter Drucker

One of the greatest pieces of economic wisdom is to know what you do not know.

John Kenneth Galbraith

I have no complex about wealth. I have worked hard for my money, producing things people need. I believe that the able industrial leader who creates wealth and employment is more worthy of historical notice than politicians or soldiers.

John Paul Getty

Money itself isn't the primary factor in what one does. A person does things for the sake of accomplishing something. Money generally follows. Owing money has never concerned me so long as I know where it would be repaid.

Colonel Henry Crown

You can delegate authority, but you can never delegate responsibility for delegating a task to someone else. If you picked the right man, fine, but if you picked the wrong man, the responsibility is yours—not his.

Richard E. Krafve

A good manager is a man who isn't worried about his own career but rather the careers of those who work for him. My advice: Don't worry about yourself. Take care of those who work for you and you'll float to greatness on their achievements.

H.S.M. Burns

Success is that old ABC—Ability, Breaks and Courage.
Charles Luckman

Humor is the lubricating oil of business. It prevents friction and wins goodwill. But Boswell says in his "Life of Johnson" that a dinner lubricates business.

Anonymous

Executive ability is the art of getting credit for all the hard work that somebody else does.

Anonymous

The harder I work, the more luck I seem to have.
Thomas Jefferson

A business with an income at its heels
Furnishes always oil for its own wheels.

William Cowper

Make it thy business to know thyself, which is the
most difficult lesson in the world.

Miguel de Cervantes

Business is like riding a bicycle—when it isn't moving
forward at a good speed, it wobbles.

Source Unknown

A pessimist sees the difficulty in every opportunity, an
optimist sees the opportunity in every difficulty.

Winston Churchill

To delegate effectively: Only do that which only you
can do.

Source Unknown

When It's Time to Say "Good-bye"

When two men in a business always agree, one of them is unnecessary. To decide which one should stay on board, ask yourself these questions:

1. Which one is more experienced and qualified?

2. Who is more willing to take on the work of an employee who is leaving in addition to his own work?

3. Who has the interpersonal skills needed to work with other employees?

Source Unknown

When an employee who has had a good record during his tenure in your company, during a meeting with you, leaves angrily, saying "I quit," and then returns the next day and asks to come back to work, what should you do?

1. Don't take any action for at least a day. This allows both of you time to think about it.

2. Discover exactly why the employee quit. Ask someone who knows the employee to find out what really triggered the outburst. Was the employee under a lot of stress, either at work or at home?

3. If the employee is sincere about coming back and is valuable to your company, let him know that walking out on the job is not an acceptable way of solving problems.

Source Unknown

I don't know anything about luck. I've never banked on it and I'm afraid of people who do. Luck to me is something else; hard work and realizing what is opportunity and what isn't.

Lucille Ball

Laziness may appear attractive, but work gives satisfaction.

Anne Frank

In democracies, nothing is more great or more brilliant than commerce.

Alexis, Comte de Tocqueville, 1849

Pity the poor businessman. When the help isn't clamoring for more pay and shorter hours, the customers are yelling for lower prices and better service.

In the business world, an executive knows something about everything, a technician knows everything about something—and the switchboard operator knows everything!

Business is like a wheelbarrow—it stands still unless someone pushes it.

Failure is not final or fatal. But not to make the attempt, that is the unredeemable failure.

It isn't the business you get that counts, it's the business you hold.

Sources Unknown

Success in Business

The essence of success is that it is never necessary to think of a new idea oneself. It is far better to wait until somebody else does it, and then to copy him in every detail except his mistakes.

Aubrey Menen

Six essential qualities that are the key to success: Sincerity, personal integrity, humility, courtesy, wisdom and charity.

Dr. William Menninger

Failure seems to be regarded as the one unpardonable crime, success as the all-redeeming virtue, the acquisition of wealth as the single worthy aim of life.

Charles Francis Adams

To burn always with this hard, gemlike flame, to maintain this ecstasy, is success in life.

Walter Horatio Pater

A minute's success pays the failure of years.

Robert Browning

How far high failure overleaps the bounds of low success.

Sir Lewis Morris

The men who succeed are the efficient few. They are the few who have the ambition and will power to develop themselves.

Herbert N. Casson

Authority without wisdom is like a heavy ax without an edge, fitter to bruise than polish.

Anne Bradstreet

Good Mental Health in Business

Your mental health will be better if you have lots of fun outside of the office.

Dr. William Menninger

Do the best job you can do today, and don't worry about what happened yesterday or may happen tomorrow.

Making a mistake is not fatal. You will have learned from your mistake and usually you will grow from your failure.

You can control how you believe and feel. If you don't like what you are feeling, make up your mind to change your thoughts to more positive ones.

Stop blaming yourself or others when things go wrong.
Instead, figure out ways to remedy the situation.

When you are having problems with another employee,
discuss your feelings with them. Don't accuse them
of being in the wrong, but let them explain their
behaviors.

Be open to suggestions from others. If the way you are
handling problems does not seem to be working, try
different solutions until you come up with a positive
approach.

Sources Unknown

Cooperation Leads to Good Teamwork

Discuss the team's goals, and make sure that team members are aware of them.

Get input from each team member. Talk about ground rules and expectations so there will not be disagreement later on. Decide on procedures.

As team leader, don't play favorites among employees. Share any accolades with the team members, rather than taking all the credit for a job well done.

Set high standards and let team members know that you expect a high level of performance. Praise them when they deserve it.

Trust the expertise and skills of other team members and respect their opinions. Show them that you believe in them. Don't overreact to mistakes.

Always keep your word. Keep all commitments you make to your employees. It's wiser to underpromise than to break your word.

When some members of the team face tight deadlines, volunteer to help out and encourage other team members not only to do their share, but to be helpful to others when needed.

Never scold or humiliate team members before the group. If reprimands become necessary, these should be administered in private.

Sources Unknown

Labor is man's greatest function. He is nothing, he can do nothing, he can achieve nothing, he can fulfill nothing, without working.

Orville Dewey

The fruit derived from labor is the sweetest of all pleasures.

Luc de Clapiers

It is only through labor and painful effort, by grim energy and resolute courage that we move on to better things.

Theodore Roosevelt

The history of the world is full of men who rose to leadership, by sheer force of self-confidence, bravery and tenacity.

Mahatma Gandhi

For they conquer who believe they can.

John Dryden

Good emotions make us well; bad emotions make us sick. What are bad emotions? Anger, hate, resentment, fear. And what are good emotions? Faith, joy, love and happiness.

Dr. Norman Vincent Peale

Two things you need for better communication: courage and safety. You need to have enough courage to both speak the truth and to make it safe for people to tell you the truth, even if it's tough for you to hear.

G. Eric Allenbaugh

The idea that there are well-rounded people who have only strengths and no weaknesses... is a prescription for mediocrity, if not incompetence. Rather than staff an organization to avoid weakness, organizations should look for strengths in their people that will meet the demands of the situation.

Peter Drucker

Real courage is when you know you're licked before you begin, but you begin anyway and see it through no matter what.

Harper Lee

Success seems to be connected with action. Successful people keep moving. They make mistakes, but they don't quit.

Conrad Hilton

Life affords no higher pleasure than that of surmounting difficulties, passing from one step of success to another, forming new wishes and seeing them gratified.

Samuel Johnson

The more we do, the more we can do.

William Hazlitt

If you have great talents, industry will improve them; if moderate abilities, industry will supply their deficiencies. Nothing is denied to well-directed labor; nothing is ever to be attained without it.

Joshua Reynolds

When you hire people who are smarter than you are, you prove that you are smarter than they are.

R.H. Grant

Employment, which Galen calls "nature's physician," is so essential to human happiness that indolence is justly considered as the mother of misery.

Richard E. Burton

Some folks can look so busy 'doing nothing' that they seem indispensable.

Kin Hubbard

About the author

From homemaker to career woman to community leader and community volunteer, Melba Sparrow's experiences encompass working in small businesses with architects, engineers and as Finance Officer for Sparrow Construction Co., Inc.

She graduated from Meredith College with a degree in Business Management, and has participated in many institutes in Raleigh and in Washington, DC. These include Small Business Institute, Managing Your Employees, Political Action and Governmental Affairs Institute, and the Governor's Conference on Leadership Development.

Currently a member of the Cary, NC Town Council and former Mayor Pro Tem, she has been an officer or an active member of Meredith College Library Board, Cary Chamber of Commerce Board of Directors and the Board of Trustees of Wake Technical Institute. She serves as a director of Triangle Bank.

In 1992, Melba Sparrow was named Outstanding Person in Community by Cary Junior Woman's Club. In 1993, she was awarded the Honorary Merit Award for Outstanding Service to the Construction Industry by the Raleigh Chapter of the National Association of Women in Construction.